ALL ABOUT THE RODEO

RODEO ROPERS

Lynn Stone

Rourke
Publishing LLC
Vero Beach, Florida 32964

www.rourkepublishing.com

Photo credits:
Front cover © Eric Limon, back cover © Olivier Le Queinec, all other photos © Tony Bruguiere except page 8 © Fred Whitfield, page 13 © Jim Parkin, page 26 courtesy of the Library of Congress, page 29 © Will LaDuke

Editor: Jeanne Sturm

Cover and page design by Nicola Stratford, Blue Door Publishing

Library of Congress Cataloging-in-Publication Data

Stone, Lynn M.
  Rodeo ropers / Lynn M. Stone.
      p. cm. -- (All about the rodeo)
  Includes index.
  ISBN 978-1-60472-389-2
 1. Calf roping--United States--Juvenile literature. 2. Steer roping--United
States--Juvenile literature. I. Title.
  GV1834.45.C34S86 2009
  791.8'40973--dc22
                                         2008018785

Printed in the USA

CG/CG

Rourke Publishing

www.rourkepublishing.com – rourke@rourkepublishing.com
Post Office Box 3328, Vero Beach, FL 32964

Table Of Contents

Rodeo Ropers

Horses, ropes, and cattle are no strangers to each other in the rodeo arena. They are as much a part of American rodeo fabric as dirt, leather, buckles, boots, and cowboy hats.

Today's professional rodeos feature seven major events. Two of them are roping events: team roping and tie-down roping. Tie-down roping used to be called calf roping. The event is the same; only the name has changed.

A rider ropes a young steer and swings down from the saddle in one fluid motion.

A tie-down roper gallops after a calf. Different rodeos use young cattle of different sizes.

A third roping event, breakaway roping, is staged largely as an event for young women in junior high, high school, and collegiate rodeos. However, the Women's Professional Rodeo Association (WPRA) holds a Women's World Finals in the event. Yet another roping contest, steer roping, is staged at a few men's competitions.

Team ropers snare a steer.

Roping events are timed. Winning is dependent upon the speed with which the competitors can complete the event. Unlike the bull riding and bronc riding events, roping events are measured strictly by time, with no attention to style.

Pigging string clenched in his teeth, a tie-down roper rushes toward a calf.

With a perfect pitch, a cowboy ropes a speeding calf.

Tie-Down Roping

Tie-down roping features a rider working with his horse, as a team, to rope a running calf. The event begins with the release of a calf into the arena. Immediately after the calf bolts into view, the cowboy and his horse chase and quickly overtake it.

With great skill the galloping cowboy tosses a rope loop around the calf's neck and brings his horse to a quick stop. As he swings down from the horse, the cowboy, with a single motion, pulls up any slack in the rope, one end of which is attached to the **saddle horn**. If the caught calf happens to run toward the horse, the horse will step back, keeping the rope tight.

On foot, the cowboy rushes to the calf. The calf is usually upright, but if not, the cowboy must wait for the calf to stand. The cowboy throws the calf to the ground and ties any of its three legs together with a **pigging string**. Tying complete, the roper raises his hands in the air to signal that he has finished the run. Meanwhile, the horse has adjusted its stance so that the rope stays just taut enough from saddle to calf so that it never drags the calf.

While riding, the cowboy grips the pigging string, a short, looped rope, in his teeth.

A cowboy wraps pigging string around three legs of the calf.

The roper returns to his horse and creates slack in the rope. The event requires that the calf must remain tied for at least six seconds. If not, the roper earns no credit for the run. Best winning times are usually in the 8 to 9 second range.

Team Roping

Team roping involves a pair of cowboys working closely together to catch a horned steer with thrown ropes.

Team ropers start their run on horseback from holding areas called **boxes** at the edge of the rodeo arena. The steer, with a brief head start, rushes into the arena from a **chute** located between the horse boxes.

A team roper in pursuit of a steer bolts from the box into the arena.

One of the two mounted ropers is a **header**. The other is a **heeler**. The header rides slightly ahead of the heeler. The header's job is to rope the steer first and to do so by one of three legal methods. His rope toss can loop around both steer horns, around the animal's neck, or around one horn and the head. If the rope catches any other location, such as the steer's nose, the run is **disqualified**.

Team ropers must loop their ropes in specific places on the steer.

After the catch, the header maneuvers the steer to turn its hind legs toward the heeler. From horseback, the heeler must then loop the steer's two hind legs. If the heeler catches just one hind leg with his rope, the team is charged with a penalty of 5 seconds.

A header ropes a steer.

The steer is still kicking its hind legs after being roped by the header. That allows the heeler to flip the rope under the steer's hind feet. The heeler is assisted by a very stiff, looped rope. Ideally, a heeler makes the catch from a very short distance, perhaps 6 feet (1.8 meters) from his arms to the steer's feet.

A heeler ropes the hind legs of a kicking steer wearing protective head gear.

After the heeler ropes the steer's hind legs, the horses step back to remove any remaining rope slack. As soon as the horses stop and face each other, the clock stops. The best team ropers finish in 5 to 6 seconds.

A heeler and a header jockey for final position at the end of a roping run.

A cowgirl casts a rope toward a running steer, its head protected by padding.

The Riders

Most tie-down and team roping events are for men, especially at the professional level. The Professional Rodeo Cowboys Association (PRCA) holds championship finals for the events each year. The WPRA does not schedule as many roping events for its women members as the PRCA does for men. However, the WPRA crowns champions in both events at its national finals.

★ Like rodeo sports in general, roping has become a popular activity at many levels of competition. Some ropers are practiced cowhands and do not try to make a living as professional ropers. A few cowboys do make a living at rodeo roping and have become dedicated to practicing the sport nearly every day, whether competing or not. The most talented professionals can earn more than $300,000 on the pro **circuit**.

Among the giants of tie-down roping history are Mike Johnson and Roy Cooper. Cooper's work included a combined eight world titles in tie-down roping, steer roping, and all-around rodeo.

The best ropers can make a living on their event.

Rich Skelton has won eight world champion titles in team roping along with former partner Speed Williams. More recently, Skelton began competing with one of rodeo's greatest all-around champions, Trevor Brazile. The Camarillo brothers, Leo and Jerold, who won six world titles together, were another legendary roping team.

Pro ropers follow a rodeo circuit, appearing at several rodeos during the year.

The Horses

Most of the horses in rodeo events are American quarter horses. Quarter horses were developed more than 100 years ago. Western cattlemen discovered they needed a sturdy, agile, and quick horse for ranching. In addition, they needed a horse with good **cow sense**. Somehow, the ideal **breed** would have keen instincts to deal with herding, chasing, and **cutting** cattle. The Westerners developed the quarter horse by crossing fast horses (called quarter-milers) from the eastern United States with Spanish mustangs from the West.

After having been brought to North America by Spanish explorers, escaped mustangs became the wild horses of the American West.

The quarter horse proved to be a natural talent for ranch and rodeo ropers.

Horse and rider work as a team to accomplish their task quickly.

The quarter horse today is an intelligent, compact, and highly versatile horse. It has earned its title of the most popular breed in America while fulfilling its many roles on working ranches. The quarter horse came with cow sense and more.

One of the quarter horse's most impressive qualities is its ability to start fast and stop quickly. That ability has endeared it to rodeo cowboys and cowgirls.

In team roping, heading horses are usually taller and heavier than heelers. The header needs plenty of strength to turn a steer. Heelers emphasize speed and agility.

A young steer runs its fastest to avoid being roped.

The History of Rodeo Roping

Rodeo sporting events originated largely from the real tasks of cowboys. Calf and steer roping are perfect examples.

Ranches of the Old West were unfenced. Cattle were free to graze over hundreds of square miles of open land. Because vegetation was often sparse, cattle had to roam to find sufficient food. Eventually, of course, ranchers had to round up the cattle. Only then could the ranch hands **brand** calves and herd their beef cattle to market.

Cowboys rode the open range in all seasons to find and herd cattle.

A cowboy lifts a small, roped calf before downing and tying it.

cfdrodeo.com

Cattle roundups required the skills of cowhands on horseback. Riding and roping were essential cowboy skills. Roping was the only practical way to collect wayward cattle and calves. Roping was also necessary to cut animals from the herd for branding.

Trucks and barbed wire eventually simplified range duties. Nevertheless, some ranches still depend upon mounted cowboys and their lariats to help maintain cattle herds. It is likely that cattle ranches will always depend upon horses, riders, and ropes to some extent. It is a *sure* thing that rodeos will!

The most skillful ropers today are in rodeo arenas.

Glossary

boxes (BOKS-iz): the holding places for horses and riders at the edge of a rodeo arena

brand (BRAND): to place an ownership stamp on livestock with a heated branding iron

breed (BREED): a particular kind of domestic animal within a larger, closely related group, such as a quarter horse within the horse group

chute (SHOOT): a tight, high-sided space in which individual animals can be contained and kept apart from each other

circuit (SUR-kit): the ongoing schedule of rodeo events from town to town

cow sense (KOU SENSS): the instinct of certain horses to anticipate the behavior of cattle

cutting (KUHT-ing): the act of a cowboy on horseback removing a cow from the rest of a herd

disqualified (diss-KWOL-uh-fide): to have been ruled ineligible for an event

header (HED-ur): a mounted cowboy who ropes a steer's head in rodeo team roping competition

heeler (HEEL-ur): a mounted cowboy who ropes a steer's hind legs in rodeo team roping competition

pigging string (PIG-ing STRING): the short rope used to tie the feet of livestock

saddle horn (SAD-uhl HORN): on a western type saddle, a knob that a rider can grasp on the upper front of the saddle

Further Reading

Want to learn more about rodeos? The following books and websites are a great place to start!

Books

Ehringer, Gavin. *Rodeo Legends: 20 Extraordinary Athletes of America's Sport.* Western Horseman, 2003.

Gabbert, Lisa. *An American Rodeo: Riding and Roping.* Rosen, 2003.

Sherman, Josepha. *Steer Wrestling and Roping.* Heinemann, 2001.

Websites

http://www.wpra.com
http://prorodeo.org
www.RopersOnly.com
www.nlbra.com

Index

About The Author

Lynn M. Stone is a widely published wildlife and domestic animal photographer and the author of more than 500 children's books. His book *Box Turtles* was chosen as Outstanding Science Trade Book and Selectors' Choice for 2008 by the Science Committee of the National Science Teachers' Association and the Children's Book Council.